Clear Cut

From Vows to Rewriting the Contract

GAIL MOORE

Disclaimer

This book is a work of nonfiction based on the author's lived experiences, reflections, and personal analysis. Certain names, identifying details, timelines, and circumstances have been changed to protect the privacy of individuals. This book is provided for informational and educational purposes only. It is not legal, financial, therapeutic, or professional advice. The author is not acting as an attorney, financial advisor, or licensed therapist in connection with this publication. Readers should seek qualified professional guidance regarding their specific circumstances. Nothing in this book creates an attorney-client, therapist-client, fiduciary, or advisory relationship between the author and the reader.

Published by Moore Clarity Consulting LLC
Atlanta, GA

ISBN: 979-8-9946652-0-6 (Paperback)
ISBN: 979-8-9946652-1-3 (eBook)
LCCN: 2026904725

First Edition
Printed in the United States of America
Cover and interior design by Gail Moore

IMPORTANT INFORMATION

This book provides general information and perspectives and should not be relied upon as legal, financial, medical, or therapeutic advice. Every divorce situation is unique and governed by specific state and local laws that vary significantly across jurisdictions. Readers are encouraged to verify any legal, financial, or emotional guidance referenced in this book with appropriately licensed professionals in their jurisdiction.

Case studies and examples in this book are either:

- Composite illustrations based on common patterns reported in family law practice
- Anonymized accounts with identifying details changed to protect privacy
- Cited from publicly available sources as indicated in footnotes

The author and publisher make no warranties or representations regarding the accuracy, completeness, or suitability of this content, and disclaim all liability for any damage, loss, or outcomes resulting from its use or reliance.

If you are experiencing domestic violence, abuse, or safety concerns, please contact the National Domestic Violence Hotline at 1-800-799-7233 or local law enforcement immediately. This book does not address situations involving abuse or safety risks.

By reading this book, you acknowledge that you understand and accept these limitations.

Dedication

To everyone who has survived love, loss, lawyers, and legal bills, this book is for you. May your future be brighter, cheaper, and filled with far fewer billable hours.

Preface

Many divorce costs are driven by avoidable decisions.[1]

Divorce can bring out the worst in even the most reasonable people. Hurt feelings, miscommunication, and unresolved resentment can turn a challenging transition into financial catastrophe. The irony is that most couples don't intend to wage war over dining tables and dog beds, but emotions often run the show, and the price tag follows.

This book explores how emotional reactions can affect decision-making in divorce. It doesn't tell you whether to divorce. It shows how unintentional choices can turn a breakup into bankruptcy. Through illustrative examples, cautionary tales, and practical strategies, these pages illustrate how clear-headed decisions matter when emotions run high.

Whether trying to save money, sanity, dignity, or all three, this book illustrates the pitfalls that can drive some divorces into six-figure territory.

How This Book Was Built

This book is not based on a single divorce story. The stories you'll read are composites, anonymized accounts, or drawn from public sources, designed to illuminate how ordinary, emotionally driven choices often trigger extraordinary financial consequences.

Over time, the same costly mistakes appear repeatedly in divorce proceedings, regardless of income level, education, or who initiated the separation.

This book distills recurring patterns into practical warnings and decision frameworks. The goal is not to tell you what decision to make, but to surface patterns of decision-making that often cost far more than they're worth.

Table of Contents

Introduction: Rewriting the Contract

Marriage can function like a contract in practical terms, even when it doesn't feel like one. It's an arrangement shaped by promises, assumptions, shared responsibilities, and legal obligations, many of which only become visible when something goes wrong. Divorce is not necessarily the failure of that contract. It is the recognition that the original terms no longer work.

When a marriage ends, the task ahead is not judgment or punishment. The reality is something far more practical, and far more demanding: **the terms are being renegotiated**.

This process is unfamiliar to most people. The language is legal. However, the emotional weight can make even straightforward choices feel overwhelming. And the outcome depends less on conflict than on clarity—clarity about assets, responsibilities, timelines, and future boundaries.

This book is not about blame, revenge, or therapy. It is about understanding how to renegotiate the terms of a shared life in a way that protects you, minimizes unnecessary damage, and allows both parties to move forward.

You may not have chosen to rewrite this contract. But you deserve to do it deliberately, intelligently, and with as much control as possible.

This is an intentionally short read that offers a practical, cautionary lens on the classic traps of divorce. It takes two to say, “I do,” but often only one determined person to send costs soaring. When emotions escalate, these pages are meant to be returned to, especially when moving on and living well matters more than prolonged conflict.

Who This Book Is For (and Who It Is Not)

This book is for readers who want to look at ways to exit a marriage with their finances, dignity, and future intact.

It is especially useful if you:

- Have assets, income, or retirement savings at stake
- Are navigating divorce later in life or after a remarriage
- Value clarity over conflict
- Prefer practical analysis to emotional reassurance
- Recognize the need for clear decision-making in emotionally charged situations

This book is not for readers seeking revenge, punishment, or moral victory. It does not promise emotional closure, validation, or courtroom triumph. It focuses on outcomes—specifically avoiding unnecessary financial destruction.

The Divorce Cost Filter

Throughout this book, you'll encounter decisions that feel urgent, justified, or necessary. Before acting on any of them, run your choice through these three questions:

- Is this emotional or strategic?
- What will this cost me financially?
- Does this move me closer to being done?

If the answer to the first question is "emotional," if the cost outweighs the benefit, or if it delays resolution—pause. Every chapter in this book will show you what happens when people don't.

You'll see this filter referenced throughout the book. Use it every time a decision feels urgent.

THE "WINNING" MINDSET

Cost Risk Snapshot: Typical financial impact of this mistake: $20,000 – $75,000, depending on duration and escalation.

Dollar figures in this book are approximate, based on typical hourly rates and ranges reported by family law practitioners and consumer legal surveys. Actual costs vary widely by state, attorney rates, and case complexity.

How Fighting to Win Guarantees Losing

Divorce has a way of convincing people that they must "win" something—custody, assets, apologies, validation, dignity—anything that proves they weren't the problem. The impulse comes from pain, not logic. And while the emotional side may crave a victory, the financial side quietly bleeds every time you react instead of plan.

Some of the most expensive divorces are not driven by complicated finances. They are often driven by hurt feelings that influence legal decisions. Wanting to win is human. Paying $40,000 to pursue it may be avoidable.

Why the Winning Mindset Is So Expensive

A divorce can become financially dangerous when you frame it as a competition. In a competition, there must be a winner and a loser. In divorce, people often experience different kinds of loss:

- You lose money
- You lose time
- You lose peace
- You lose momentum in rebuilding your life

When both spouses try to "win," attorneys may spend more time preparing for conflict than for resolution. Every email is more pointed. Every motion is more aggressive. Every negotiation is more rigid. The divorce becomes a chess match played with checkbooks.

And here's the part most people don't realize: Even if you "win," you may spend more on the war than what you won is worth. That is the trap.

Signs You've Slipped into Win-Mode

You might be in the winning mindset if:

- You reject reasonable offers because they feel insulting
- You want the judge to see their true character
- You're focused on principle instead of outcome
- You feel satisfaction imagining your ex being inconvenienced
- You want the final agreement to sting—just a little

These reactions are common, and they can also be expensive.

What a Healthy Divorce Mindset Looks Like

A healthy mindset isn't about being passive, but rather strategic.

A strategic mindset asks:

- What matters most to me?
- What can I let go of?
- What gets me closer to being done?
- What protects my financial future—five, ten, twenty years from now?

A strategic mindset understands that:

- Settling isn't losing
- Compromise isn't weakness
- Efficiency is a financial skill
- Bitterness is budget poison

The Real Goal: Resolution, Not Victory

A divorce is not usually a criminal trial. It's not a boxing match. It's not a place for revenge assignments or reputation repair. It is a legal and financial uncoupling.

The goal is not to win. It is to finish well.

Finishing "well" means:

- You get a fair agreement
- You protect your money and credit
- You prevent unnecessary conflict
- You preserve your mental health
- You move on faster

Winning is emotional. Finishing well is practical.

Practical Steps to Avoid the Winning Mindset

What You Want vs What You're Trying to Prove

Ask yourself: "Is this about the issue, or is this about my feelings?" If it's the feelings, don't send it to your attorney yet.

Get a Hard Number from Your Lawyer

Before fighting over any point, ask: "How much will it cost me to argue about this?" Compare that number to what you're arguing about. If the math doesn't make sense, the fight doesn't either.

Pick Your Top Three Priorities

Not ten. Not seven. Three. When everything is a priority, nothing is.

Use Your Attorney Strategically

Your attorney is a legal resource. Use them to execute strategy, not create it. Ask what something will cost, and stay focused on outcomes rather than emotional wins.

Focus on Your Future Self

Picture yourself one year from now. What will matter? The $1,200 couch? The vacation points? The "principle"? Probably not. But your savings account, credit score, and peace of mind certainly will.

Real-World Example

A couple spent seven months and $40,000 in combined attorney fees arguing over a $3,200 tax refund.[2] By the time the judge ordered them to split it, they'd spent the refund more than ten times over. Each wanted to "win" the principle. Neither wanted to compromise. The result? Both lost far more than they could have gained.

Case Study: Marcus

Marcus wanted to "teach his wife a lesson" by rejecting every settlement proposal.[3] Nine months later, her attorney fees had doubled—and so had his. Marcus eventually agreed to the original settlement offer. His need to "win" cost him an additional $35,000 and nearly a year of his life. When asked what he accomplished, Marcus had no answer.

Closing Perspective

You cannot control your spouse's behavior during divorce. But you can control whether you feed the fire or walk away from it. The legal process often works better when parties cooperate and stay efficient, rather than escalating conflict.

When you let go of the need to win, you create the space to resolve. You save money. You save time. You save yourself from unnecessary chaos.

A divorce doesn't need a winner. It needs two people willing to end the story without writing a financial tragedy.

Worksheet: Identify Your Triggers

Take a moment to reflect on these questions:

- What issues make you feel the need to "win"?

  ____

  ____

  ____

- What outcome do you really want?

  ____

  ____

  ____

- Does fighting help you reach it, or delay it?

  ____

  ____

  ____

- If you spent $10,000 on this issue, would you feel good about that decision a year from now?

  ____

  ____

  ____

The Numbers Don't Lie

Tom and Jennifer had $180,000 in marital assets. Tom insisted on "fighting for what's mine." After 18 months of litigation, the judge awarded him $95,000, which was approximately 53% of the total. His legal fees totaled $47,000. Jennifer's attorney fees (which he was ordered to partially cover) totaled $18,000.

Net result

Tom walked away with $30,000. He spent $65,000 in combined legal fees to "win" 3% more than a 50/50 split would have given him. Meanwhile, his first settlement offer, which he rejected eight months earlier, would have netted him $85,000 after minimal legal costs.

The winning mindset cost Tom $55,000.

THE $5,000 SOFA WAR

Cost Risk Snapshot: Typical financial impact of this mistake: $3,000 – $15,000 per item, depending on duration and escalation.

Fighting Over Stuff Costs More Than the Stuff

There's something about divorce that transforms ordinary household items into symbols of justice, validation, and victory. That dining table? It's not just furniture anymore. It's proof that you contributed to the marriage. The sofa? It represents all the compromises you made. The air fryer? Well, you picked it out.

This is how a $600 sofa becomes a $5,000 legal battle.

The emotional weight we attach to objects during divorce rarely matches their actual value. But attorneys bill by the hour, and arguing about property takes time—lots of it. Emails, phone calls, negotiations, court filings, and sometimes even professional appraisals. Before you know it, you've spent more on the fight than you could spend replacing everything you're fighting over.

The Psychology of Property Division

When a marriage ends, people often fixate on tangible items because they feel like something they can control. You can't control the divorce. You can't control your spouse's behavior. You can't control how you feel. But you can fight for the couch.

Channeling emotional pain into something concrete is a displacement behavior. The problem is that judges, attorneys, and mediators often recognize it as: an expensive distraction from the real issues.

Common patterns include:

- **Sentimental attachment:** "That was my grandmother's china." (Even if you never used it.)
- **Fairness obsession:** "I paid for it, so I should keep it." (Even though you're also splitting a mortgage.)

- **Punishment motivation:** "They don't deserve it." (Even though it means you don't get it either.)
- **Principle over pragmatism:** "It's the principle of the thing." (Principles are expensive.)

The True Cost of Fighting Over Property

Let's break down what it actually costs to fight over household items.

Attorney Time

- Emails about the item: $75-$150 per exchange
- Phone calls discussing strategy: $200-$400 per call
- Drafting formal requests: $300-$600
- Court motions if unresolved: $1,500-$3,000

Other Costs

- Professional appraisals: $150-$500 per item
- Storage fees if contested: $100-$300 per month
- Emotional toll and delayed resolution: Priceless (but actually very expensive)

Reality check: A $600 sofa may generate $3,000 in legal fees if both parties dig in. A $2,000 dining set? Try $8,000 in costs. And that's just for one item.

Real-World Example

A couple litigated over a $600 sofa for eleven months.[4] The husband claimed he bought it. The wife claimed she picked it out and it matched her new apartment. Neither would budge. By the time they appeared in court, they had racked up:

- 47 emails between attorneys
- 6 phone conferences
- 1 formal motion filed
- 1 appraisal (which valued it at $400 used)
- Combined legal fees: $4,200

The judge ordered them to sell the sofa and split the proceeds. They netted $200 each. Between the attorney fees and storage costs, the fight cost them more than a quick getaway vacation.

Case Study: Nina and the Dining Table

Nina wanted the dining table "on principle." Her ex wanted it because Nina wanted it.[5] What started as a simple property division item became a symbol of their entire marriage. Nina argued she hosted all the family dinners. He argued he paid for it.

Six months and $6,800 in legal fees later, they were both exhausted. Nina's attorney finally asked her: "Do you want to be right, or do you want to be done?"

Nina let it go. Her ex took the table. Three months later, he sold it on Facebook Marketplace for $300. Nina bought a new one she liked better for $450.

Lesson learned: Sometimes the "win" isn't worth the war.

How to Divide Property Without Going Broke

Here's a practical framework for handling property division.

1. Separate items into three categories:

- **High-value items:** Vehicles, jewelry, art, collectibles (worth negotiating)
- **Sentimental items:** Family heirlooms, photos, personal effects (usually easy to split)
- **Everything else:** Furniture, appliances, household goods (not worth fighting over)

2. Apply the replacement cost test:

- **Before fighting over any item, ask:** "How much would it cost to replace this?" If you can replace it for less than $500, it's almost never worth arguing about. If legal fees to fight over it would exceed replacement cost by 3x or more, walk away.

3. Use the "you pick, I pick" method:

Take turns selecting items from a shared list. This eliminates the endless back-and-forth negotiations. It's fair, efficient, and dramatically reduces attorney involvement.

4. Document everything:

Create a shared spreadsheet listing all property, estimated values, and who takes what. Get written agreement. This prevents future disputes and shows the court you tried to cooperate.

5. Let go of "winning":

If your spouse wants something badly enough to fight over it, consider whether letting it go is worth the savings. The goodwill you create may pay dividends in other negotiations.

ATTORNEYS ARE NOT THERAPISTS

Cost Risk Snapshot: Typical financial impact of this mistake: $5,000 – $25,000, depending on duration and escalation.

Why Legal Bills Reflect Emotional Processing

Divorce is emotionally devastating. You're dealing with betrayal, grief, anger, fear, and uncertainty—sometimes all in the same day. You need to process these feelings. You need to talk through what's happening. You need someone to listen.

Your attorney is not that person, and treating them as one quietly converts emotional processing into billable time.

It's not that they don't care—many genuinely do. But their job is to provide legal strategy, not emotional support. And when you use them for the latter, you pay $300-$500 per hour for what should be a $150 therapy session or a free conversation with a friend.

The Billable Hour Reality

Many attorneys track their time in increments, often 6-minute blocks or 15-minute blocks. Everything counts.

- Phone calls (even the ones where you "just had a quick question")
- Emails (reading, drafting, replying)
- Text messages (yes, even these)
- Document review
- Research and strategy
- Court appearances
- Travel time to/from meetings

For example, at $400/hour, a 30-minute "venting session" would cost $200. A 2-hour call where you process your feelings costs $800. Five such calls and you've spent $4,000 on emotional support that accomplished nothing legally.

What Your Attorney Should Actually Do

Your attorney's role is to:

- Explain your legal rights and obligations
- Develop strategy for asset division and custody
- Draft and file necessary documents

- Negotiate with opposing counsel
- Represent you in court if necessary
- Provide realistic assessments of your case
- Protect your interests within the bounds of the law

Notice what's not on this list: validating your feelings, listening to stories about your spouse's behavior, discussing your emotional state, or helping you process the end of your marriage.

Real-World Example: John's $15,000 Venting

John called his attorney 2-3 times per week for six months.[6] Most calls lasted 45 minutes to an hour. The conversations typically involved John venting about his ex's behavior while his attorney listened professionally. Cost per call: $300-400. Total over six months: $15,000. Legal progress made: Zero.

John's attorney was professional and responsive. But John was using a $400/hour legal professional as a sounding board. When John finally got his bill, he was shocked. "I didn't realize talking costs so much."

How to Use Your Attorney Efficiently

Here's how to work with your attorney in a cost-effective way.

Prepare Before You Contact Them

Before calling or emailing, write down the specific legal issue or question, relevant facts (dates, amounts, who said what), what you need from them (advice, action, filing), and any supporting documentation.

Batch Your Questions

Instead of calling every time you think of something, keep a running list. Schedule one call per week (or as needed) to address multiple items at once. This is far more efficient than five separate 15-minute calls.

Send Concise Emails

Structure emails with a clear subject line, brief opening, relevant facts only (3-5 sentences max), and specific questions. Convert a two (2) page narrative with no clear question into five (5) sentences stating the issue and asking for specific guidance.

Distinguish Between Legal and Emotional Issues

- Legal issues: custody violations, missed support payments, property access disputes, filing deadlines.
- Emotional issues: how you feel about your ex, processing grief, managing anger.

If it's emotional, talk to a therapist. If it's legal, contact your attorney.

Respect Their Time (and Yours)

If your attorney says, "I need to research this," let them. Don't follow up three hours later asking if they've made progress. Trust that they're working on your case.

Set Communication Boundaries

Establish a communication plan early. How often should we communicate? What constitutes an emergency? What's the expected response time? Can a paralegal handle routine questions to save costs?

Who Should You Talk To Instead?

When you need emotional support, consider these resources:

- **Therapist or counselor:** often $100–$200 per session, depending on location and provider

- **Divorce support group:** Often free, peer support, shared experiences
- **Divorce coach:** $75-$150 per session, practical guidance without legal advice
- **Trusted friends/family:** Free, available, emotionally supportive (but choose wisely)
- **Online forums:** Free, anonymous, but verify information with professionals

For example, 10 therapy sessions may cost about $1,500–$2,000, while 10 hour-long attorney calls for venting may cost $4,000–$5,000.

Closing Perspective

Divorce is legitimately one of the most painful experiences you'll ever go through. You absolutely need emotional support. You need someone to listen. You need help processing what's happening.

But get that support from the right people. Your attorney is a legal strategist, not a therapist. Using them as the latter is expensive, inefficient, and ultimately unhelpful.

Build a proper support team: attorney for legal matters, therapist for emotional processing, friends for day-to-day venting. This approach saves you money, gets you better outcomes, and actually helps you heal.

The Therapy Bill Disguised as Legal Fees

Michelle called her attorney 3-4 times per week throughout her 10-month divorce. Most calls lasted 20-45 minutes. She discussed her ex-husband's new girlfriend, her own dating anxieties, her mother's opinions about the divorce, and her fears about the future. Her attorney listened patiently and offered general life advice.

When Michelle's final bill arrived, she was shocked to find $18,500 in charges labeled "client communications." At $350/hour, her emotional processing sessions had cost more than most people spend on an entire divorce.

Meanwhile, a licensed therapist charging $150/hour would have provided better emotional support for $6,000, and her sessions would have been protected by therapeutic privilege, not discoverable by opposing counsel.

Every dollar you save on inappropriate attorney communication is a dollar you can invest in your new life. Use it wisely.

THE HIDDEN COST OF HIDING MONEY

Cost Risk Snapshot: Typical financial impact of this mistake: $25,000 – $250,000+, depending on duration and escalation.

When "Clever" Becomes Catastrophically Expensive

Some people think they're being smart by hiding assets during divorce. They open secret accounts. They underreport income. They transfer money to family members. They invest in cryptocurrency thinking it's untraceable. They stash cash in safe deposit boxes.

Here's what they don't realize. Hiding assets doesn't just risk discovery; it often increases the chance of discovery. And when (not if) those assets are found, the financial and legal consequences far exceed whatever was hidden.

Forensic accountants are very good at their jobs. Courts don't appreciate being lied to. And the penalties for hiding assets can destroy what you were trying to protect.

Why People Hide Assets

The motivations are usually:

- **Fear:** "They'll take everything from me."
- **Revenge:** "They don't deserve half of what I earned."
- **Distrust:** "The system isn't fair."
- **Entitlement:** "I earned it, it's mine."
- **Desperation:** "I need to protect myself and the kids."

These feelings are understandable. Hiding assets is not a solution.

How Assets Get Discovered

Forensic accountants and opposing attorneys have multiple tools to uncover hidden assets:

- Bank statements and transaction histories
- Tax returns and W-2s/1099s
- Credit reports and credit card statements
- Business records and financial statements
- Real estate records and property deeds
- Retirement account statements

- Digital payment trails (Venmo, PayPal, Zelle, Cash App)
- Cryptocurrency exchange records (not as anonymous as you think)
- Lifestyle analysis (court compares spending to declared income)
- Depositions under oath
- Subpoenas to financial institutions
- Private investigators if warranted

Reality: If you touched it electronically, it may be traceable. If you spent it, you left a trail. If you earned it, there's a record. The digital age makes hiding money much more difficult.

The Real Costs of Hiding Assets

When hidden assets are discovered, you face:

- **Forensic accounting fees:** $5,000–$50,000+ depending on complexity—you may end up paying for both sides
- **Additional attorney fees:** $10,000-30,000+ for the extended litigation
- **Court sanctions:** Financial penalties imposed by the judge
- **Adverse judgment:** You may lose more in the division than you would have lost honestly
- **Criminal charges:** In extreme cases, perjury or fraud charges

- **Damaged credibility:** Once caught lying, your testimony on everything else is suspect
- **Contempt of court:** Fines, attorney fee awards to the other side, even jail time
- **Tax consequences:** IRS may be notified of unreported income

Real-World Example: The $18,000 Crypto Wallet

A software engineer thought he was clever by converting $18,000 to cryptocurrency and keeping it in a hardware wallet.[7] He didn't disclose it in his financial affidavit. His ex-wife's attorney noticed his tax return showed a capital gain from crypto sales. A subpoena to the exchange revealed the full history.

Outcome: Forensic accounting fees: $8,500. Additional attorney fees: $12,000. Court sanctions: $5,000. He had to give his ex-wife the entire $18,000 plus pay her attorney fees for the discovery. Total cost of hiding $18,000: $43,500.

Case Study: The Underreported Freelance Income

Maria ran a freelance consulting business and regularly received cash payments. She reported only 60% of her actual income to reduce child support obligations.[8] Her ex-husband's attorney conducted a lifestyle analysis comparing her declared income to her spending, mortgage payments, and social media posts showing vacations.

The discrepancy was obvious. The court ordered retroactive child support based on her actual income, plus penalties. Then the IRS got involved. Between back child support, attorney fees, tax penalties, and interest, Maria paid more than $60,000, far exceeding what she saved by underreporting.

Closing Perspective

Hiding assets is a terrible strategy for three reasons: it usually fails, the penalties are severe, and it damages your credibility on everything else.

Courts understand that divorce makes people anxious about money. They expect some disagreement about values and division. What they don't tolerate is dishonesty.

Full disclosure may feel scary, but it's the only path forward that doesn't risk catastrophic consequences. Work with your attorney to protect your interests legally. Don't try to cheat the system.

The temporary satisfaction of "getting away with it" isn't worth the permanent damage when you're caught.

WHEN KIDS BECOME LEVERAGE

Cost Risk Snapshot: Typical financial impact of this mistake: $50,000 – $200,000+, depending on duration and escalation.

The Most Expensive Mistake Parents Make

IMPORTANT: This chapter addresses custody disputes motivated by conflict, not safety concerns. If there are genuine issues of abuse, neglect, or danger to children, this guidance does not apply. Prioritize children's safety and consult appropriate professionals. When abuse, coercion, or danger is present, you must seek appropriate help.

Nothing in this chapter should be interpreted as minimizing legitimate safety concerns. Financial efficiency never outweighs personal safety or a child's wellbeing.

Using children as leverage in divorce is one of the fastest ways to destroy your finances, damage your kids, and lose the respect of everyone involved, including the judge.

Parents do this for many reasons: hurt, revenge, control, and fear. But regardless of the motivation, using custody to punish your ex or win the divorce is devastating on every level.

Family court judges have seen many manipulation tactics. They often recognize when custody demands are about the children's best interests versus when they're about hurting the other parent. And they respond accordingly.

How Parents Use Kids as Leverage

Common tactics include:

- Demanding sole custody when joint custody would work
- Fighting over every hour of the parenting schedule
- Withholding visitation to punish the other parent
- Making false or exaggerated allegations
- Refusing reasonable compromises on schedules
- Using the kids as messengers or spies

- Bad-mouthing the other parent to the children
- Arranging events that conflict with the other parent's time
- Threatening to move away with the children

These tactics can harm children, and they are often expensive. None of them will make you look good in court.

The Financial Cost of Custody Battles

Contested custody cases are often among the most expensive divorce proceedings because they can involve:

- **Attorney fees:** $15,000 – $50,000+ per parent
- **Guardian ad litem:** $5,000 – $15,000 (attorney appointed to represent children's interests)
- **Custody evaluations:** $3,000 – $10,000 (psychological assessments)
- **Expert witnesses:** $2,000 – $8,000 each
- **Multiple court hearings:** $1,500 – $3,000 per appearance
- **Mediation attempts**: $1,000 – $5,000
- **Modification motions:** Additional $5,000 – $15,000 each time

Total potential cost for a protracted custody battle: $50,000 – $150,000+ combined. And that's before considering the emotional toll on everyone involved.

The Emotional Cost to Children

Many studies suggest that ongoing parental conflict can be more harmful to children than divorce itself. High-conflict custody battles can cause:

- Anxiety and depression in children
- Behavioral problems at school and home
- Difficulty forming healthy relationships
- Academic struggles
- Loyalty conflicts causing emotional distress
- Long-term trust issues

The financial costs are often outweighed by the developmental and psychological harm to children caught in the middle.

Case Study: The 50/50 War

A father demanded exactly 50/50 custody, not because it was best for his kids, but because it would reduce child support and upset his ex-wife.[9] She refused, citing the children's school schedule and activities. Both dug in.

Over 14 months, attorney fees exceeded $75,000 combined. A custody evaluator cost $7,500. Guardian ad litem fees cost $12,000. The kids underwent multiple interviews and assessments. Their grades dropped. Their anxiety increased.

The judge's final ruling: 60/40 custody (close to what mom originally proposed), child support calculated accordingly, both parents ordered to take a co-parenting class.

The father spent $40,000 to get 10% less time than if he'd accepted the initial proposal. The children spent over a year in limbo while their parents fought.

What Courts Actually Care About

Judges often make custody decisions based on the child's best interests, considering:

- Each parent's ability to meet the child's physical and emotional needs
- The child's existing relationships with each parent
- Stability of each home environment
- Each parent's willingness to support the child's relationship with the other parent
- The child's preference (depending on age and maturity)
- Any history of domestic violence, abuse, or neglect
- Each parent's mental and physical health
- Geographic proximity and practical logistics

Notice what's NOT on this list: who was wronged in the marriage, who earns more money, who initiated the divorce, or who "deserves" the kids more.

How to Protect Your Kids (and Your Wallet)

If you genuinely want what's best for your children:

Put kids first, not hurt feelings

Start by basing custody proposals on what actually works for the children's schedules, relationships, and needs, instead of what punishes your ex.

Default to reasonable sharing

Unless there's a safety issue, both parents often should be meaningfully involved. Fighting over hours is usually about control, not children.

Keep kids out of the conflict

Never use them as messengers. Don't ask them to choose sides. Don't bad-mouth the other parent. Shield them from adult problems.

Be flexible

Kids' needs change. Schedules need adjustment. Rigidity helps no one. The parent who demonstrates flexibility often gets more cooperation.

Document appropriately

If you have genuine concerns about safety or neglect, document them properly and report to appropriate authorities. Don't weaponize minor parenting differences.

Consider the long game

You'll be co-parenting for years, potentially decades. Every battle now affects that future relationship. Choose cooperation over conflict when possible.

Closing Perspective

Your children didn't choose this divorce. They didn't ask for their family to be split. They deserve parents who prioritize their wellbeing over hurt feelings and revenge.

Every dollar you spend on an unnecessary custody battle is a dollar taken from your kids' future. Every hour spent in court is an hour not spent actually parenting. Every moment of conflict is another moment of damage.

Be the parent your kids need, not the parent your anger wants you to be. It's the right thing to do, and it's far, far cheaper.

The $80,000 Custody War Nobody Won

Robert and Lisa had two children, ages 7 and 10. Both were fit parents. Both wanted primary custody. Neither would compromise. The battle required two custody evaluations ($12,000 each), a guardian ad litem ($25,000), four expert witnesses ($18,000 combined), and extensive depositions and court time ($40,000 in legal fees).

The outcome

The judge ordered a 50/50 custody split—the exact arrangement their mediator had suggested 14 months earlier for a $3,000 fee.

The real cost

Beyond the $107,000 in combined expenses, both children developed anxiety disorders requiring therapy. The 10-year-old told her counselor she wished her parents had "just figured it out" instead of making her talk to all those strangers about private stuff. Neither parent won. Both children lost.

Apply The Divorce Cost Filter

Tom spent $65,000 fighting for 3% more. Robert and Lisa spent $107,000 fighting for custody they both already had. The pattern is identical—emotion driving decisions, and lawyers billing by the hour.

SKIPPING MEDIATION

Cost Risk Snapshot: Typical financial impact of this mistake: $30,000 – $100,000+, depending on duration and escalation.

The $30,000 Shortcut You Can't Afford to Skip

Mediation is often the most cost-effective way to resolve divorce disputes, yet many couples skip it or approach it in bad faith. This chapter explores why mediation works, how much it saves compared to litigation, and how to prepare for successful mediation.

Judges often encourage mediation not because it is easier, but because it consistently produces outcomes that align more closely with court-imposed resolutions at a fraction of the cost.

Key points: Mediation may cost about $2,000–$8,000 total, compared with roughly $30,000–$100,000 for contested litigation in many cases. Some programs report settlement rates around or above 70% when both parties participate in good faith. Even partial agreements in mediation can dramatically reduce trial costs.

Mediation makes sense when both parties are willing to communicate, have no safety concerns, and have relatively equal bargaining positions. When those conditions are not present, alternative legal approaches may be necessary.

How to succeed in mediation

Prepare financial documents thoroughly, identify priorities vs. preferences, bring realistic expectations, listen to understand not just to respond, and focus on interests rather than positions.

Real-World Example: The $30,000 Shortcut

A couple was $15,000 apart on a final property settlement. The husband, feeling insulted, refused mediation, stating he wanted his "day in court" to prove his wife was being unreasonable.

- **The Path Taken:** They spent the next 14 months in litigation.

- **The Cost:** Between depositions, multiple court hearings, and trial preparation, they spent a combined $60,000 in additional legal fees.
- **The Result:** The judge eventually ordered a settlement nearly identical to the last offer made before the trial.
- **The Lesson:** They spent $60,000 to argue over $15,000. Mediation could have resolved this in one afternoon for a fraction of the cost.

THE $10,000 SOCIAL MEDIA POST

Cost Risk Snapshot: Typical financial impact of this mistake: $5,000 – $20,000, depending on duration and escalation.

How Your Digital Life Becomes Court Evidence

Anything you post online may be used in divorce proceedings. That vacation photo, that angry tweet, that check-in at an expensive restaurant, it all becomes evidence. This chapter shows how social media destroys divorce cases and what to do about it.

Common mistakes

Posting about new relationships while separated, displaying spending inconsistent with financial affidavits, venting about your ex publicly, sharing details about the case, posting photos that contradict testimony (claiming depression while posting happy vacation photos).

The discovery process

Attorneys routinely subpoena social media records. Even deleted posts may sometimes be recoverable. Screenshots can persist long after a post is deleted. Your friends' posts can expose you too.

Safe social media during divorce

Consider going dark entirely. If you must post, assume the judge will see it. Never post about the case, your ex, or the proceedings. Never post financial information. Adjust all privacy settings (but know they're not foolproof).

Case Study: Sarah's "Girls' Trip"

Sarah claimed in court that she was financially destitute and required maximum spousal support.

The Mistake

Two weeks before the final hearing, she posted photos from a luxury resort in Mexico with the caption, "Living my best life, finally free!"

The Discovery

Her ex-husband's attorney introduced the screenshots as evidence.

The Consequence

The judge found Sarah's testimony regarding her financial need to be not credible.

The Financial Hit

Not only was her alimony request significantly reduced, but she was ordered to pay $10,000 of her husband's legal fees because her dishonesty unnecessarily prolonged the discovery process.

THE REBOUND RELATIONSHIP

Cost Risk Snapshot: Typical financial impact of this mistake: $10,000 – $30,000, depending on duration and escalation.

Why Dating Too Soon Costs More Than Dinner

Starting a new relationship during divorce proceedings can complicate custody arrangements, increase conflict, provide ammunition to opposing counsel, and drain emotional bandwidth that you'll need for the divorce process itself.

How new relationships complicate divorce

Opposing counsel may imply affairs (even if relationship started after separation), new partners can be called as witnesses, and judges may view new relationships unfavorably when children are involved. It provides emotional ammunition that escalates conflict.

The timing question

Many people choose to wait until the divorce is finalized before starting a new relationship. At minimum, wait until you're legally separated and have filed. Don't introduce children to new partners until the relationship is serious and stable. Don't bring new partners to custody exchanges or court appearances.

The emotional reality

You're not emotionally ready as soon as you think you are. Divorce takes longer to process than people expect. Rebound relationships rarely last. Take time to heal before adding another person to your life.

Real-World Example: The New Roommate Penalty

David began dating and moved his new girlfriend into his home while the divorce was still pending.

The Legal Complication

His ex-wife's attorney immediately filed a motion to restrict David's overnight visitation with the children, citing "concerns about the stability of the environment" and the presence of a stranger.

The Financial Drain

This triggered a mandatory custody evaluation and a guardian ad litem investigation.

The Cost

David spent $12,000 in expert fees and an additional $8,000 in legal fees defending his right to have his girlfriend present during his parenting time.

The Lesson

Waiting until the ink was dry on the divorce decree would have saved David $20,000 and months of high-conflict litigation.

UNREALISTIC EXPECTATIONS

Cost Risk Snapshot: Typical financial impact of this mistake: $20,000 – $50,000, depending on duration and escalation.

What TV Taught You Wrong About Divorce Court

Many people enter divorce with unrealistic expectations about what courts will do, how judges make decisions, and what constitutes "fair." Managing expectations prevents expensive disappointment.

Common unrealistic expectations: "In many no-fault jurisdictions, the judge may care less about infidelity than the legal issues at hand", "I'll get the house because I want it more" (not how it works),

"They'll have to pay for their behavior" (divorce isn't about punishment), "My attorney will fight for me to win everything" (good attorneys manage expectations).

What judges actually consider

Judges must consider state law and legal precedent, financial facts and documentation, what's practical and enforceable, children's best interests (not parents' preferences), and equal treatment under the law.

Setting realistic expectations

Consult with your attorney early about likely outcomes. Understand your state's laws on property division and support. Accept that fairness may not match your feelings. Recognize that compromise isn't losing, it's resolving.

Case Study: The Infidelity Tax That Doesn't Exist

Karen was determined to take everything because her husband had been unfaithful. She instructed her lawyer to reject any offer that didn't give her 80% of the marital assets as punishment for his behavior.

The Reality Check

Her attorney warned her that their state was a no-fault jurisdiction where the judge would likely divide assets 50/50 regardless of the affair.

The Cost of Ignorance

Karen fired her first lawyer for not being aggressive enough and hired a high-conflict firm.

The Result

After spending $45,000 in legal fees and a two-day trial, the judge split the assets 50/50, exactly as the first lawyer predicted.

The Lesson

Karen's emotional expectation of "justice" cost her nearly $50,000 of the very assets she was trying to protect.

Unrealistic expectations do not just lead to disappointment—they lead to prolonged litigation. Courts move on facts, not narratives. The faster expectations align with legal reality, the faster financial bleeding stops.

DEATH BY A THOUSAND CUTS

Cost Risk Snapshot: Typical financial impact of this mistake: $50,000 – $145,000+, depending on duration and escalation.

How Small Decisions Add Up to Financial Devastation

It's rarely one big mistake that makes divorce expensive. It's the accumulation of dozens of small, emotionally driven decisions. This chapter synthesizes the lessons and provides a framework for decision-making.

The pattern of escalation

It starts with one emotional reaction. Then another. Then another. Each seems justified in the moment. But cumulatively, they transform a $15,000 divorce into a $100,000 nightmare.

The decision-making framework

Before taking any action, ask: Is this legal or emotional? Will this move me closer to resolution? What will this cost vs. what will I gain? How will I feel about this decision in one year? Would I advise a friend to do this?

Breaking the cycle

Recognize emotional triggers before you act on them. Build in waiting periods for major decisions. Use your support team (therapist, friends) before contacting your attorney. Remember that done is better than perfect. Focus on your future, not your past.

Real-World Example: The "Daily Update" Bill

James was anxious and called his attorney every morning for a status update, even when there were no pending deadlines.

The Billing Pattern

Each 10-minute call was billed at a minimum increment of 0.25 hours ($100 at his lawyer's $400 hourly rate).

The Accumulation

Over the course of a year, James made approximately 150 of these "quick" calls.

The Total

When the final bill arrived, James found he had spent $15,000 just on status updates that provided no legal value to his case.

The Lesson

By not batching his questions or using a paralegal for routine info, James bled his savings dry through minor, impulsive decisions.

Epilogue: The Cost of Peace

Divorce is not a failure. It's a transition. And while transitions are painful, they don't have to be financially devastating. When you choose clarity over chaos, cooperation over conflict, and strategy over emotion, you preserve more than money—you preserve your future.

Every lesson in this book comes down to one principle

You cannot control your spouse, the legal system, or even many aspects of the divorce itself. But you can control how you respond. You can choose to escalate or de-escalate. You can choose resolution over revenge. You can choose to spend your resources fighting or rebuilding.

Many of the most expensive divorces are not complicated; they are emotional. The least expensive divorces aren't easy, they're intentional. The difference is choice.

Choose to protect your children instead of using them as weapons. Choose therapy over venting to your attorney. Choose to let go of things that don't matter. Choose to focus on outcomes instead of principles. Choose to be done rather than to be right.

The goal isn't to avoid divorce at all costs. It's to avoid costs that don't serve your healing, growth, or stability. Whether you're walking into a courtroom, a mediator's office, or simply into a new phase of life, choose peace. It's the cheapest, healthiest, and most powerful choice you can make.

Your new life is waiting. Don't spend it all in divorce court.

References and Notes

[1] American Psychological Association. (2023). Divorce. https://www.apa.org/topics/divorce-child-custody

[2] Illustrative composite example. See Note on Illustrative Examples below.

[3] Illustrative composite example. See Note on Illustrative Examples below.

[4] Illustrative composite example. See Note on Illustrative Examples below.

[5] Illustrative composite example. See Note on Illustrative Examples below.

[6] Illustrative composite example. See Note on Illustrative Examples below.

[7] Illustrative composite example. See Note on Illustrative Examples below.

[8] Illustrative composite example. See Note on Illustrative Examples below.

[9] Illustrative composite example. See Note on Illustrative Examples below.

Bibliography

American Psychological Association. (2023). Divorce. https://www.apa.org/topics/divorce-child-custody

American Academy of Matrimonial Lawyers. (2022). Survey of current trends in family law. https://www.aaml.org

Association for Conflict Resolution. (2022). About mediation. https://acrnet.org/page/AboutMediation

Nolo. (2024). How much will my divorce cost? https://www.nolo.com/legal-encyclopedia/how-much-will-my-divorce-cost.html

National Center for State Courts. (2023). Family court statistics quarterly. https://www.ncsc.org/information-and-resources/research/court-statistics

Internal Revenue Service. (2024). Innocent spouse relief (Tax Topic 205). https://www.irs.gov/taxtopics/tc205

Note on Illustrative Examples

Footnotes [2] through [9] reference illustrative composite examples. These are not drawn from any single identifiable case or individual. Each scenario is a constructed illustration built from patterns that recur across published family law sources, practitioner accounts, and publicly documented court proceedings. They are included to illustrate behavioral and financial patterns common in contested divorce, not to document specific legal cases or outcomes.

Published sources consulted in the development of illustrative examples include: Nolo, "How Much Will My Divorce Cost?" (2024); American Academy of Matrimonial Lawyers annual cost surveys; Divorce Magazine, various issues on property division and custody disputes; and family law practitioner commentary published in state bar journals.

Note on Financial Estimates and Cost Data

Dollar figures appearing in Cost Risk Snapshots, chapter examples, and the “Cost of Emotional Decisions” summary table are approximate estimates based on ranges reported by family law practitioners and published consumer legal surveys, including those from the American Academy of Matrimonial Lawyers and Nolo. Actual costs vary significantly by state, jurisdiction, attorney hourly rates, and case complexity. All figures should be treated as illustrative ranges, not guarantees of likely expense in any specific proceeding.

Mediation settlement rate figures cited in this book ("around or above 70%") reflect ranges commonly reported across state court ADR programs and professional mediation organizations, including the Association for Conflict Resolution. These rates vary by jurisdiction, program design, and participant commitment. Readers seeking jurisdiction-specific data should consult their state court's alternative dispute resolution office or the National Center for State Courts.

How to Use This Book During Your Divorce

This book is not meant to be read once and shelved. It's a tool to use when emotions spike and decisions feel urgent.

- Read one chapter when emotions spike—not to calm down, but to see the cost before you act.
- Use emotional check-in worksheet before contacting your attorney to filter emotional urgency from strategic necessity.
- Revisit Cost Risk Snapshots before making demands or rejecting offers.
- Apply The Divorce Cost Filter to every decision that feels justified by principle.
- Stop reading once you're calm again. The goal isn't to memorize chapters, it's to interrupt expensive impulses.

Use this book as a circuit breaker between emotion and action. That pause is where you save money.

If You Remember Only Three Things

If you remember nothing else from this book, remember this:

1. Emotional decisions are the most expensive ones you will make in divorce.
2. Being right is rarely worth the price of proving it.
3. Finishing well is usually cheaper than fighting longer.

Divorce is not where you win, it is where you exit. The goal is not victory. The goal is to preserve enough of your resources, health, and momentum to build what comes next.

Emotional Check-In Worksheet

Use this worksheet before making any major divorce decision:

- What am I feeling right now?

  ____

  ____

  ____

- What triggered this feeling?

  ____

  ____

  ____

- Is this about the current issue or past hurts?

  ____

  ____

  ____

- Do I need legal advice or emotional support?

  ____

  ____

  ____

- Can I wait 24 hours before acting on this feeling?

  ____

  ____

  ____

- Have I talked to my therapist/support system about this?

  ____

  ____

  ____

- What would I advise a friend in this situation?

  ____

  ____

  ____

State Resources & Legal Guidance

Divorce laws vary significantly by state. This book provides general guidance, but you must consult with an attorney licensed in your jurisdiction.

To find legal resources in your state

- State Bar Association websites offer lawyer referral services.
- Legal Aid organizations provide free/low-cost assistance based on income.
- Court self-help centers offer forms and procedural guidance.
- Law school clinics sometimes offer supervised representation.

Key state law differences to research

- Community property vs. equitable distribution states
- Fault vs. no-fault divorce requirements
- Residency requirements for filing
- Child support calculation methods
- Spousal support (alimony) guidelines
- Custody presumptions and standards

The Cost of Emotional Decisions

The following is an illustration of the financial consequences of choosing emotional reactions over strategic decisions.

Scenario	The Emotional Choice	The Strategic Choice	The Emotional Tax (Loss)
Mediation	Refusing a $15,000 gap to get a day in court.	Settling via mediation for $5,000 total fees.	$55,000+ in unnecessary legal fees.
Social Media	Posting luxury vacation photos to "feel better."	Staying dark on social media during the case.	$10,000+ in sanctions and lost support.
Dating	Moving in a new partner immediately.	Waiting until the divorce is finalized.	$20,000+ in custody evaluations and GAL fees.
Legal Expectations	Hiring a "shark" to punish an unfaithful spouse.	Accepting "no-fault" 50/50 reality early.	$45,000+ for a predictable outcome.
Communication	Daily "status update" calls for anxiety relief.	Batching questions for one weekly call.	$15,000+ in billable "venting" time.
TOTAL POTENTIAL LOSS:		**$145,000+**	

As demonstrated, the cumulative cost of emotional decision-making can easily transform a modest divorce into a six-figure financial disaster. Each choice may seem justified in the moment, but the long-term consequences are profound.

About the Author

Gail Moore is a seasoned writer with extensive experience in translating complex topics into practical, accessible guidance. With a background in technical communication and knowledge management, she brings clarity, humor, and insight to one of life's most challenging transitions.

Drawing on personal experience, extensive research, and consultations with legal and mental health professionals, Gail created this guide to help others avoid the costly mistakes that turn divorce into financial catastrophe.

She believes that while divorce is painful, it doesn't have to be bankruptcy-inducing, and that with the right guidance, people can emerge from divorce financially intact and emotionally prepared for their next chapter.

This book was written to help readers recognize costly patterns early before emotional decisions turn manageable divorces into financial disasters.

www.ingramcontent.com/pod-product-compliance
Lightning Source LLC
LaVergne TN
LVHW011048110826
845149LV00015B/3407
9798994665206